"All over this nation, God is stirring the hearts of men to rise up and enter into their God-given destiny. Lou Turner's lifelong passion is to see men enter into their divine purpose in life. 'Living Life God's Way,' of which this book is a part, is born out of this passion. Throughout this Bible study series, Turner opens up God's Word to help you discover HIS plan for your success in your life, family, and work. If you are ready to get off the treadmill, to begin to enjoy God's fullness in your life and make a significant contribution to the world around you, I recommend that you dive into this life-transforming Bible study."

Hal H. Sacks, D.Min., *BridgeBuilders International Leadership Network*

"It seems North American culture is rapidly moving toward what the Bible calls 'everyone doing what is right in his own mind' (Judges 21:25). The prophet Isaiah declared, 'Woe to those who call evil, good, and good, evil' (Isaiah 5:20). This Bible study series will challenge every man in the 21st century as 'iron sharpens iron'! The Q&As at the end of each chapter really personalize the teaching."

Dennis Conner, *Co-Founder/President, Called to Serve Prayer-Coaching Ministry*

"I have known Lou Turner for over twenty years. Lou loves Jesus and has built his life on the Word of God. Lou's Bible study series, 'Living Life God's Way,' is full of biblical truth that has been tested and can be applied by disciples of Jesus in practical ways. These books will help you grow in your faith and gain confidence and competence, which will increase your fruitfulness in Christ.

Mark Buckley, *Founding Pastor of Living Streams Church*

Living Life God's Way

Getting Guidance from God

Lou Turner

Getting Guidance from God
First Edition, 2020
Copyright © 2020 by Lou Turner

Getting Guidance from God is part of of the Living Life God's Way Series by Lou Turner.

All rights reserved. No part of this publication may be reproduced, stored in a retrieval system, or transmitted in any form by any means—electronic, mechanical, photocopy, recording, or otherwise—except for brief quotations in critical reviews or articles, without the prior permission of the publisher, except as provided by U.S. copyright law.

Unless otherwise identified, Scripture quotations are from the ESV® Bible (The Holy Bible, English Standard Version®), copyright © 2001 by Crossway, a publishing ministry of Good News Publishers. Used by permission. All rights reserved.

Scriptures marked NKJV are taken from the New King James Version., copyright 1982 by Thomas Nelson. Used by permission. All rights reserved.

Some of the anecdotal illustrations in this book are true to life and are included with the permission of the persons involved. All other illustrations are composites of real situations, and any resemblance to people living or dead is coincidental.

ISBN: 978-1-7329092-8-1

To order additional books:
www.hislifeinus.com
www.amazon.com

Editorial and Book Packaging: Inspira Literary Solutions, Gig Harbor, WA
Cover Design: MTWdesign, Dickson, TN
Typesetting: PerfecType, Nashville, TN

Printed in the USA by Ingram Spark

He will be like a tree firmly planted by streams of water,
Which yields its fruit in its season
And its leaf does not wither;
And in whatever he does, he prospers.

Psalm 1:3

TABLE OF CONTENTS

Preface   ix

How to Use This Book   xi

Introduction   xiii

1. Pursue Wisdom   1

2. Seek God in Prayer   11

3. How God Speaks   23

4. Confirmation and Timing   35

A Final Word   45

About the Author   47

PREFACE

We live in a world that has largely forgotten what manhood is about. In the Western world, men are often portrayed on television as buffoons who are out of touch and must rely on their wives to straighten them out. These characters are portrayed as silly, insensitive, lacking common sense, and when they do speak, they are generally wrong. They are generally portrayed as either ridiculously weak or overly macho. They are not able to commit to a long-term relationship and generally mistreat women. Positive role models are hard to find in the media.

However, the Bible teaches a different type of manhood, the authentic one. Men are to be leaders, loving their wives and children, excelling in their work, and standing for truth. They are to be men of wisdom, knowledge, having godly character and seeking after God and His direction. They are to be exhibiting godly leadership at church, in the community, and in business, and to be a light to those around them. They are to be men of compassion and love, as well as courageous and bold when needed.

Men go astray from these ideals, including Christian men, due to improper convictions or beliefs about life. They have received these from various sources: well-meaning family and friends, the media, and the culture around them—a world system that promotes the tearing down of God's biblical truths.

But without proper biblical foundation, we will all go astray.

PREFACE

That's why I wrote these books, containing insights, observations, and biblical truths distilled over the course of my decades of life and ministry. Each section is designed to be a stand-alone section for study and consideration. I hope this series, *Living Life God's Way*, will be used to disciple men in biblical truths for life. Whether you use it for yourself, with a group, or to mentor or disciple someone else, my hope is that it will be a blessing to you and encourage you to seek God and grow in Him.

HOW TO USE THIS BOOK

What does it mean to be a "good" husband and father?
How do I live out the Christian life at work?
What does God want from me—and how am I supposed to find that out?

These were questions that plagued me as a young man—questions, I learned, that are at the front of many men's minds at various times in their lives. For me, these questions began my quest to seek God and discover the answers, and my discoveries, over the years of my life, led to this series of booklets, *Living Life God's Way*. The series discusses 13 topics that every man must deal with, regardless of his work, calling, profession, or circumstances. It is difficult to know how to live the Christian life without understanding what God says about these areas of life.

These topics are:

1. Seeking and Finding God
2. Who You Are in Christ
3. A Man's Work and Ministry
4. Understanding Authority
5. A Man and His Wife
6. A Man and His Children
7. Getting Guidance from God

HOW TO USE THIS BOOK

8. Overcoming Strongholds
9. A Man and Money
10. Repentance, Forgiveness, and Restitution
11. Being a Leader
12. A Man and Sex
13. The Test of Pride

You can use these books to study on your own, in a small group, or with a larger group of men. Each topic or booklet is a stand-alone study, and a person can begin with any one he chooses. They are different lengths and can be adapted to various settings—home, church, or community—all topics that are pertinent to today.

Explore what the Bible says about these important and critical areas. The encouragement is to read these with an open heart, asking God to reveal His truth to you in each of these areas of life. Pray that His Spirit will show you His truth, so that you may live in it and enjoy all God has for you. I pray that you experience the blessing and presence of God in your life as you draw closer to Him and more aware of His leading in every area of your life.

INTRODUCTION TO GETTING GUIDANCE FROM GOD

Make me to know your ways, O LORD; teach me your paths. Lead me in your truth and teach me, for you are the God of my salvation; for you I wait all the day long.
(Psalm 25:4-5)

We all make decisions daily. Most of them are simple, and the right choice seems obvious. At other times, whether we realize it or not, we are making a life-changing decision, such as when we choose a mate or a career path. Important decisions about jobs, families, finances, churches, new opportunities, financial risks, and many other areas can have deep and profound effects that will influence our futures. Certainly, we all have made poor decisions that have turned out anywhere from bad to disastrous. So, trying to make good decisions is vital.

As followers of Christ, it is important to obtain direction from the Lord regarding our lives. Not going to Him can open us up to being misled or deceived. He promises to give us both wisdom and direction if we seek Him for it. *"For the LORD gives wisdom; from his mouth come knowledge and understanding; he stores up sound wisdom for the upright; he is a shield to those who walk in integrity"* (Proverbs 2:6-7).

God's Word clearly tells us that He is *"the rewarder of those who diligently seek him"* (Hebrews 11:6). We all need guidance, direction, and the ability to make good decisions, and God has promised to give us what we need. These are great and meaningful promises, and we should take them to heart!

This is an important topic, so let's prayerfully get into it.

Chapter 1

Pursue Wisdom

I was young and full of ambition. A man came along with a business opportunity full of potential to make a lot of money and do some significant things. He promised success and prestige, which of course I wanted. The fact that he claimed to be a Christian and we would be doing everything for God's glory was the icing on the cake. I jumped into the opportunity, convinced God must have opened this door for me.

I worked hard, yet the money wasn't coming in. My bills were going unpaid and I was struggling to keep food on the table for my wife and children. Even so, I proudly told people God was leading me and the outcome would eventually be very, very good.

I finally realized that my own heart's desires had been leading me, and my family was suffering as a result. I had to make a change. I was pursuing a dream and not God's direction for my life. My pride was wounded, my wife was hurt, my credit was damaged, and I was confused. How could this have happened?

Naturally, making important decisions can be critical and stressful. We can be convinced we're following God and yet be lacking in discernment. God does put dreams into our hearts and vision into our lives, but we can also pursue things in our own way and not according to God's timing or direction. Obtaining God's direction is not always quick and easy, but He promises to reveal Himself to us if we will seek Him and not give up.

The Basics

From a practical viewpoint, the first step in making good decisions is to gather the necessary information so you can to consider all sides of the topic. Jesus said,

> *For which one of you, when he wants to build a tower, does not first sit down and calculate the cost to see if he has enough to complete it? Otherwise, when he has laid a foundation and is not able to finish, all who observe it begin to ridicule him, saying, "This man began to build and was not able to finish." Or what king, when he sets out to meet another king in battle, will not first sit down and consider whether he is strong enough with ten thousand men to encounter the one coming against him with twenty thousand? (Luke 14:28-31)*

Even though Jesus was not speaking here about a decision-making process, He did highlight general wisdom regarding plans. We should:

- contemplate the options
- calculate the cost
- consider the resources

For anyone, Christian or not, this is a good practice. Many times, the right decision will become clear as we do this.

Look at all sides—the positive and negative, the "up" side (potential benefits) and the "down" side (potential risks). The more important the decision, the greater the need for due diligence in fact gathering to make the most informed decision possible. After you have gathered the information, pray over it, and ask God for direction. Get godly counsel, if needed, and wait until you feel a peace in your spirit before you decide.

These practical basics are a good guide for making important decisions. Often these steps will help us make the right decision.

God's Wisdom

Seeking God's guidance means we start with God's wisdom for all of life.

In the first nine chapters of Proverbs, the Lord emphasizes repeatedly that we need to look to Him for wisdom. If you have never carefully read Proverbs 1–9, please take time to do so. Read these chapters, meditate on them, and consider how they apply to you. They will bring life to your soul and insight to your thinking. For now, we will focus on a portion of Proverbs 2, which says,

> *My son, if you receive my words and treasure up my commandments with you, making your ear attentive to wisdom and inclining your heart to understanding; yes, if you call out for insight and raise your voice for understanding, if you seek it like silver and search for it as for hidden treasures, then you will understand the fear of the LORD and find the knowledge of God. For the LORD gives wisdom; from his mouth come knowledge and understanding; he stores up sound wisdom for the upright; he is a shield to those who walk in integrity. (Proverbs 2:1-7)*

This passage tells us a number of important things:

Be willing to receive. First, we must be willing to receive God's words and wisdom. Sometimes people say they want direction from God when they actually want His blessing for the direction they've already decided to take. Asking God for direction means our hearts are open to *His* direction—which may be different from ours (see Isaiah 55:8-9).

Treasure God's commands. Second, we are blessed when we treasure His commands, or His Word, and obey them. Psalm 1 says a man is blessed when "*his delight is in the law of the Lord, and on His law he meditates day and night.*" As we meditate on God's Word ("plant" it into our hearts and minds), it will guide us. Then, we will be "*like a tree planted by the rivers of water, that brings for its fruit in its season, whose leaf also shall not wither.*" Whatever this man does "*shall prosper*" (see Psalm 1:1-3). Knowing and following the teachings of God's Word will cause our works to succeed and lead us to avoid evil. As we "delight" in His word (go to it for truth and direction), it will bring us wisdom (see Psalm 119:105).

When I read God's Word, I pray before I begin and ask God to speak to me through it. I often pray over what I am reading and ask God to make the truth I read real in my own life. I ask Him for understanding when I do not fully understand the passage. Often, I will stop and think about a passage and contemplate what it means to me. I don't try to hurry through my Bible reading time (just so I can check the box—"Okay, I've done that") because my desire is to feed on His Word.

Cry out to God. Proverbs 2 also tells us we are to "cry out" to God for discernment, understanding, and wisdom. When the Bible speaks of "crying out," it is talking about praying to God and sincerely, earnestly, asking Him for something. Much of what we receive from God after accepting Jesus into our lives comes from seeking Him. He wants us to pursue Him and then He responds to us—this is a biblical pattern. He desires to give us what we need but wants us to come to Him to receive wisdom, guidance, and direction.

We will miss out on much of what the Lord has for us if we don't seek Him for it

Fear the Lord. Finally, when we do these things, we *"will understand the fear of the* L<small>ORD</small>*, and find the knowledge of God"* (Proverbs 2:5). As we study God's Word with an open heart, we come to realize that His truth is real. We also come to understand that there can be consequences for not seeking and following Him. We can be led astray and be deceived by things that sound good or look good on the surface; we need God to lead and guide us. This realization brings the fear of the Lord—a proper respect and awe of Him.

The translation of the word "fear" used here is the Hebrew word *yirah*, which translates "awe and respect." We are to have a proper respect and awe of God. As His children, we do not need to be "afraid" of Him; this is not the kind of fear this passage is talking about. We can run to Him as our loving Father, but also have a holy distrust of ourselves without His guidance.

It is important to understand God's love and grace and also to understand the "fear of the Lord." Just as parents want their children to know how much they are loved and cherished, parents also want their children to have a "fear" or healthy respect for the consequences of disobedience. This is part of parents' safeguards and protection for their beloved children.

We are to rest in God's love and grace, knowing it is always there for us as His children. Being convinced of God's love brings a security and peace nothing else can. (For more on this, please read the study in this series, *Who You Are In Christ*.) At the same time, a wholesome fear of the Lord brings godly caution and a deep desire to flee from evil and sin, and their consequences.

Many people fall into sin because they have no wholesome fear of the Lord. Their attitude is, "God loves me and will forgive me." While that is true, it is also true that God may discipline us for wrong attitudes and sinful actions. He will do it out of love and for our good, to train us and change our hearts and attitudes so we will desire to serve Him more earnestly. God said of His people, *"And I will make an everlasting covenant with them, that I will not turn away from doing them good; but I will put My fear in their hearts so that they will not depart from Me"* (Jeremiah 32:40).

We must understand that His ways are best and to be desired. If we are disregarding His truth and ways, we will not obtain His best. The fear of the Lord is a healthy fear, not an unhealthy one.

Ask for His resources. Along with wisdom, Proverbs 2 tells us of other qualities, or treasures, we should ask God for. They include knowledge, discernment, insight, understanding, prudence, and discretion. This is a great list. We need all of these things, and if we have them, we will be ahead of the game, so to speak. We should not be shy about asking God for these qualities and gifts. We should seek for and ask for all of these because we really need them. We should boldly ask the Lord for all of these, as He desires to give them to us. If we have these, they will help equip us to navigate everyday life. God desires and delights for us to ask for these qualities, and He desires and delights to give them to us.

Wisdom for All of Life

Proverbs tells us that searching out wisdom is not only for when an important decision is looming. We are to constantly desire wisdom, that we may be wise in all things at all times. As we become wise from seeking God, we will make wise decisions.

James 1 states that we are to ask God for wisdom and to ask in faith believing that He will respond. *"But if any of you lacks wisdom, let him ask of God, who gives to all generously and without reproach, and it will be given to him"* (James 1:5).

Far too often, Christians seek God only in a crisis and not in daily life. Thus, they are far more susceptible to making bad decisions that can cost them dearly. Certainly, we are to cry out to God in times of crisis, whether they result from bad decisions or from circumstances beyond our control. God will show Himself faithful and strong on our behalf (Psalms 107:6,13,19,28). However, if we are constantly making bad decisions because we are unwilling to take the time to search out God's wisdom, at some point He may allow difficult circumstances to continue until we have a change of heart and are willing to pursue Him.

But know this, He is always with us and is prepared to step in and help us through all situations as we turn to Him.

Ways God Leads Us

God desires us to be discerning because He wants the best for us. Wisdom from God's Word and from His work in our lives will give us insight and lead to understanding that will help keep us from bad choices. The Lord uses different methods to give us His guidance:

Through the Bible. The Bible directs us in how to live. A wise person reads it daily for insight, understanding, and spiritual strength. The Bible addresses the subjects of marriage, raising children, handling money, associations and friendships, business ventures, relationships, the future of mankind, and every other topic important in life. It is filled with wisdom and knowledge, treasures and insight.

Understanding God's will for our lives begins by meditating on what He has written. Meditating simply means to ponder it, what it means, and how it applies to our lives. It's hard to do this if we are always in a hurry. We need to take time to be still before the Lord and allow Him to work in our life.

God also instructs us to study His Word. *"Do your best [study] to present yourself to God as one approved, a worker who has no need to be ashamed, rightly handling the word of truth"* (2 Timothy 2:15). We cannot accurately handle God's Word without knowing it. I've found that if I begin each time of Bible reading by asking God's Spirit to speak to me as I read, I get far more insight and direction from Him.

In addition, one of the ways we should check out our decisions or direction is by whether or not they agree with God's Word. If we do not know His Word, we won't be able to do this and are more apt to make bad decisions. God never leads us contrary to the truths of His Word.

Through others. The Bible tells us we should look for wise guidance from others. *"A wise man will hear and increase in learning. And a man of understanding will acquire wise counsel"* (Proverbs 1:5). Pride will lead us to thinking we don't need input from others, but God doesn't want us to be spiritual islands. As Christians, we are part of God's Church and His body of believers. We are to consult others when appropriate and be open to God speaking to us through others. While we may not need counsel for all decisions, we certainly will for some.

I have received insight and direction from numerous people: from my wife, my children, men of God, pastors, employers, employees, friends, authors, even unbelievers. You may say, "Wait a minute, God doesn't want us to get advice from unbelievers. He doesn't speak through them." On the contrary, God may choose to give you direction in any number of ways. I have received good counsel numerous times from men who are wise in practical things even though they are not Christians. While I would not look to unbelievers regarding areas where they would have no knowledge of biblical truth, there may be areas in which they are wise.

No matter who gives it, all guidance should be compared with Scripture; make sure it is scripturally sound. Sometimes, as we talk with others, things may become clear and we may get all the direction we need. At other times, we may get pieces of the puzzle that will come together later as we pray about the matter.

Through prayer. God tells us to pray and to persist in prayer (Luke 18). Jesus often spent all night in prayer, talking with His Father (Luke 6:12). In the next chapters, we will discuss in more depth how we seek God in prayer and how He speaks to us in His still, small voice.

QUESTIONS FOR REFLECTION AND DISCUSSION

1. When are you likely to look for others' counsel? In what additional areas might it be helpful to do so?

   _____

   _____

   _____

2. Consider whom you could go to for counsel: Do you have wise men to talk with? If you are married, do you ask your wife for counsel? List below the people you go to for advice, wisdom, and help when you need discernment.

   _____

   _____

   _____

3. In daily life, in what ways do you "cry out" to God for wisdom and making decisions?

_____

_____

_____

4. Do you seek God by daily Bible reading and ask Him to give you wisdom and guide you? If not, what holds you back? Think about it realistically and be honest. Write your thoughts below.

_____

_____

_____

TAKE A KNEE

Let's kneel before the Lord and pray. If you are unable to kneel, do so in your heart.

"Father, I realize that in order to receive wisdom from You, I need to humble myself and admit I truly need it. I am not adequate within myself to go through life in the manner I should. I need You. I confess my need. I need Your wisdom and guidance daily. Draw near to me and show me Your ways."

Chapter 2

SEEK GOD IN PRAYER

Prayer is talking to God and spending time with Him. It is an essential part of the Christian life and the Bible encourages us to pray often and to be in an attitude of prayer at all times: "... *pray continually, give thanks in all circumstances*" (I Thessalonians 5:17,18). This is not speaking of actually being *in prayer* at all times. That would be impossible if we are working and doing other things that require us to concentrate on our tasks and interact with others. What the apostle Paul likely means here is that we should have an awareness of being before God at all times, in His presence, and trying to honor Him.

"Praying at all times" is also trying to be constantly aware of and sensitive to God's Spirit. We can pray as we go about our daily activities and ask God for His guidance, direction, and help. It is about communing with Him and trying to share our lives with Him always. This habit is something we can practice and become better at as we do so. But another important aspect of prayer is the time we set aside to be alone and pray and seek Him. The more regularly we spend time in prayer—whether focused time alone with Him or as we are going about our day—the more likely we are to receive guidance from Him as we are open to receiving His guidance.

Jesus communed regularly with His heavenly Father in prayer, sometimes even spending all night talking with Him (Luke 6:12). During these times, He received the direction He needed, strength for what lay ahead, and the joy of His Father's presence. Jesus is our example in this. He said,

Truly, truly, I say to you, the Son can do nothing of Himself, unless it is something He sees the Father doing; for whatever the Father does, these things the Son also does in like manner. (John 5:19)

We also should strive to do what our heavenly Father would have us do. We can be confident that He desires to show us His will and will empower us to do it. One way He shows His will and purpose for us is through His promptings during our times of prayer.

Ask, and it will be given to you; seek, and you will find; knock, and it will be opened to you. For everyone who asks receives, and he who seeks finds, and to him who knocks it will be opened. Or what man is there among you who when his son asks for a loaf, will give him a stone? Or if he asks for a fish, he will not give him a snake, will he? If you then, being evil, know how to give good gifts to your children, how much more will your Father who is in heaven give what is good to those who ask Him! (Matthew 7:7-11)

Prayer is not some mystical, magical thing that is hard to master. It is talking to God about our lives, looking to Him for help, asking for wisdom and direction, presenting our needs and others' needs to Him, and spending time thanking and praising Him. Things happen as we pray—real results. We should think of prayer as the lubrication that unleashes the activity of the Holy Spirit. God responds to our prayers, though not always in the way or the time we think He should.

The Spirit's Still, Small Voice

I was with a small group of men and asked them if God had ever spoken to them. Most said He hadn't. As we discussed this, it became apparent they believed that when God spoke, it was in an audible voice. Since they had not heard Him audibly, then God hadn't spoken.

While Scripture does record times when God spoke audibly or by sending an angel with His message, that is not the most common way God speaks or communicates. Very few Christians have heard God audibly. When it happened in Scripture, it usually marked an important event and God wanted no doubt regarding what He was saying. I described this to the men, and then we discussed the many ways God communicates to our hearts and minds.

At times, as we are quiet and still before God during prayer, we will sense the Holy Spirit's presence and hear His still, small voice speaking to us through thoughts and impressions. He may give us direction, reveal things about our hearts and lives, give insight into Scripture, or share His heart. These are precious, valuable, and life-changing times.

An example of this is found in 1 Kings. Elijah the prophet had just won a major victory for God that demonstrated to Israel, by an impressive miracle, that God was real. Afterward, the wicked queen Jezebel threatened to kill Elijah, and he ran for his life into the wilderness. He came to a cave, where God spoke to him.

> *"What are you doing here, Elijah?"*
> *He said, "I have been very jealous for the* L<small>ORD</small>*, the God of hosts. For the people of Israel have forsaken your covenant, thrown down your altars, and killed your prophets with the sword, and I, even I only, am left, and they seek my life, to take it away."*
> *And he said, "Go out and stand on the mount before the* L<small>ORD</small>*." And behold, the* L<small>ORD</small> *passed by, and a great and strong wind tore the mountains and broke in pieces the rocks before the* L<small>ORD</small>*, but the* L<small>ORD</small> *was not in the wind. And after the wind an earthquake, but the* L<small>ORD</small> *was not in the earthquake. And after the earthquake a fire, but the* L<small>ORD</small> *was not in the fire. And after the fire the sound of a low whisper.*
> *And when Elijah heard it, he wrapped his face in his cloak and went out and stood at the entrance of the cave. And behold, there came a voice to him and said, "What are you doing here, Elijah?" (1 Kings 19:9-13)*

Sometimes, we think God's answers to our prayers should come through some great demonstration. While God can communicate to us in spectacular manners, He usually speaks to us in His gentle voice as we are quiet and still before Him.

There have been times in my own life when the Lord has spoken to me and revealed life-changing truths. I will never forget a time when the Lord revealed that my attitudes toward my wife were wrong. I realized I had hurt her many times due to my hardness of heart and pride. As the Lord showed me this, I was crushed with sadness and remorse. I repented and asked God to change me and show me how to love my wife as He wanted me to. Our relationship began to change from that time.

Another time as I was praying, God revealed I was not walking in the freedom He had for me. I began to see several areas where my life was not lining up with Scripture. I had grown accustomed to living this way and had come to accept it. However, God showed me I did not have to settle for less than His will and scriptural promises. I began to ask Him to change my heart, renew my mind, and teach me to walk in freedom. I felt convicted that I needed to pray over these areas daily, sometimes several times a day. As I did, my heart began to change, my thinking began to change, and my life began to change in those areas.

It was a gradual process that happened as I sought God and prayed. By opening my heart and seeking God, and seeking Him earnestly and diligently, I began to see change and freedom come. God could have done it immediately, but He wanted me to seek Him and believe for change. During that time, I gained insights and understanding I didn't previously have. God was doing a work in my life and life change was taking place.

These truths were revealed to me as I sought God and desired to be open to Him. God wants to reveal His truth and abundant life to us (John 10:10). He loves us and wants us to live in freedom from sin and bondage and live our lives as overcomers. As we diligently come to Him with an open heart, He will reveal Himself, His truth, and His direction.

Prayer with Fasting

In addition to seeking God through prayer, there are times when we will want to both pray *and* fast as we come to Him. Fasting is not often spoken of in some circles. However, it is biblical, and we are encouraged to do it. Prayer with fasting can lead to God revealing obstacles or bondages in our lives that need to be broken in order for Him to guide us into what He has for us. Jesus spent time in fasting (see Matthew 4). If He needed to do so, then we might also!

Medically, there are physical benefits to fasting; it can help purge our bodies. But the Bible speaks of fasting in order to hear from God or break bondage in our lives or to intercede for others' lives. During fasting, we become more sensitive to hearing from God, and our hearts are often more open to Him. Personally, at times I have received meaningful or even life-changing direction from God while fasting.

One passage that speaks of the purpose of fasting is Isaiah 58:6-12:

> *Is not this the fast that I choose: to loose the bonds of wickedness, to undo the straps of the yoke, to let the oppressed go free, and to break every yoke? Is it not to share your bread with the hungry and bring the homeless poor into your house; when you see the naked, to cover him, and not to hide yourself from your own flesh?*
>
> *Then shall your light break forth like the dawn, and your healing shall spring up speedily; your righteousness shall go before you; the glory of the Lord shall be your rear guard. Then you shall call, and the Lord will answer; you shall cry, and he will say, "Here I am."*
>
> *If you take away the yoke from your midst, the pointing of the finger, and speaking wickedness, if you pour yourself out for the hungry and satisfy the desire of the afflicted, then shall your light rise in the darkness and your gloom be as the noonday. And the Lord will guide you continually and satisfy your desire in scorched places and make your bones strong; and you shall be like a watered garden, like a spring of water, whose waters do not fail. And your ancient ruins*

shall be rebuilt; you shall raise up the foundations of many generations; you shall be called the repairer of the breach, the restorer of streets to dwell in.

There is a lot to unpack in this passage. It tells us that during a fast, God wants us to seek Him to break bondage (bring release and freedom) and establish justice, to be motivated to take care of our families and the poor, and to act properly toward others.

I encourage you to read and meditate on this chapter and its meaning. The truth it contains is important and meaningful and can give direction for your life, whether or not you are fasting.

When we draw close to God in prayer and fasting, He may want to deal with our actions and attitudes toward others. Often, when we get that right, the blessings and direction He has for us will follow. More than once when I was seeking God, I was impressed to take actions that led to God's "next step" for me. At times there was an obstacle to my moving forward that needed to be cleared, so I could move ahead.

One weekend, I was away in prayer and fasting as I went to God for direction. I woke up on Saturday and the Spirit of God was convicting me of a direction I had taken in my local church, where I was an elder. I was deeply impressed that I had wronged church leadership by my words and actions, and that I had led a number of others to do the same. Please understand that at the time, I had thought I was doing the right thing. But I had not sought the Lord as I should have, especially considering the number of people my actions would affect. I acted more on impulse as I tried to fix a problem through my own understanding.

I made a list of people I knew had taken my bad counsel. When I got back home, I began to call them and confess my bad decision, and ask for forgiveness. I also called those who had been in leadership with me and confessed how the Lord convicted me.

Then, with the pastor's permission, the following Sunday I got up in front of the church, confessed my wrongdoing, and asked for forgiveness.

Numerous broken or strained relationships were restored. I had to humble myself, but the result was restored relationships—plus increased wisdom not to make the same mistake again. Any ministry I would have hoped for in that church would have been greatly compromised until this had been done. God was more concerned about me getting things right with others than answering what was on my mind at that time.

I began my prayer time making petition for one thing, but God had something else in mind that was much more important, much like Jesus spoke about when He said, *"Therefore, if you are offering your gift at the altar and there remember that your brother has something against you, leave your gift there in from of the altar. First go and be reconciled to your brother; then come and offer your gift"* (Matthew 5:23-24).

Often doors will open after we discern God's will and obey His leading. As you read Isaiah 58, note what God wants to accomplish in your life and the promises that are yours as you seek God through prayer and fasting. If you are considering a time of fasting, it would be worthwhile reading and praying over this chapter to see if God might impress things upon you through His Word. God's agenda is often different than ours. He may want us to get to the place that we desire in our hearts, but the path may be different than we think.

If we are praying and seeking God and He seems to be silent, then that means we should wait until we get a confirmation to move forward or go a different direction. There are times to move full steam ahead and times to stop and wait. Until we have peace (and in the case of important decisions, confirmation of His direction), we should wait. Fasting can sometimes help bring about the confirmation and peace we are seeking from God through prayer.

Practicalities

Biblically, fasting is always spoken of as abstaining from food. A person might fast for one meal, a day, or longer. Practically, fasting can mean eating no food and only drinking water, or it can mean eating only those foods required to give us energy and abstaining from any "pleasant foods." This is the type of fast Daniel did when he prayed, fasted, and waited for three weeks for an answer to things that were troubling him (Daniel 10:2-3).

Some people, such as diabetics, may be unable to fast for physical reasons. If this is the case with you, a fast with juices or limited food may enable you to fast. You can consult with your doctor about this.

Please understand: Prayer, not merely abstaining from food, is the purpose for fasting. During a time of prayer and fasting, a person can read God's Word or biblically based books, pray, and ask God for direction. During these times, we should open our hearts to hear whatever God may want to communicate. It may be correction, encouragement, or direction. Sometimes I do not get God's answer during the fast but receive it in the days or weeks to follow. If you have a critical decision to make, are having a difficult time with an area of your life and feel stuck, or feel drawn to have a special time with God, consider fasting for a meal or a day and spend that time with God. It may change your life!

I have gone away for personal weekend retreats for the purpose of prayer and fasting. At times, I have had specific things I wanted to pray about. At other times I have just wanted to seek God, enjoy His fellowship, and open myself to hear from Him. Sometimes, when I have had specific things on my heart, I haven't always gotten the answer during the time of prayer. Often God had other things in mind that were on His agenda (and not necessarily mine).

Be assured, seeking God through prayer and fasting brings results. They may not always what you have in mind, but they will be what God has in mind. Prayer is a vital and essential practice for every Christian, and I encourage you to set aside time for prayer daily. The enemy will try to side track you and keep you from prayer. Resist! (James 4:7) Persevere, remembering that practicing prayer reaps great rewards: *". . . . for he who comes to God must believe that He is, and that He is a rewarder of those who diligently seek Him"* (Hebrews 11:6, NKJV).

QUESTIONS FOR REFLECTION AND DISCUSSION

1. Have you ever set aside time to fast and pray? If so, how long did you fast? What was the result?

   _____

   _____

   _____

   _____

2. If you have fasted in the past, have you done so recently? Can you think of any reasons to set aside a time to seek God for things on your heart? If so, what are they?

   _____

   _____

   _____

   _____

3. What type of fast do you think would work best for you? (A simple way to fast is to skip one meal a week and during that time to pray and seek God.)

_____
_____
_____
_____

4. Have you set aside time for prayer and seeking God, even if you did not fast? What was the result?

_____
_____
_____
_____

TAKE A KNEE

Let's pray: *"Dear Father, You promise that You will reveal Your will and purposes to me as I seek You. You also promise to break any bondages or clear any hindrances in my life, which can lead to Your being able to use me more in Your kingdom. Draw me to You in prayer. If You desire me to set aside time for prayer and fasting, impress that upon me. I trust You and know You have only good for me."*

Chapter 3

How God Speaks

God communicates, or speaks to us, by His Spirit. Jesus said, *However, when He, the Spirit of truth, has come, He will guide you into all truth; for He will not speak on His own authority, but whatever He hears He will speak, and He will tell you things to come. He will glorify Me, for He will take of what is Mine and declare it to you. (John 16:13-14)*

The Holy Spirit's communication can come to us in different forms. Often, the Spirit speaks by thoughts and impressions. When people say God "spoke" to them, this is usually what they mean. God gives thoughts and impressions to our minds and spirits to give direction and reveal what He desires us to know.

In my own experience, when I am praying or studying God's Word, God's Spirit will begin to impress things upon me—or "quicken" thoughts to me, as some might say—in order to communicate. Many times this will be direction regarding things I am praying about, insights about the Scriptures I am reading, or God communicating His heart or will to me about some matter.

God can also speak to us through dreams and visions. Both the New and Old Testaments include accounts of men and women receiving dreams and visions from the Lord. In the book of Genesis, Joseph had a number of dreams that revealed God's purpose for his life. God then used others' dreams, which had significant meanings, to demonstrate that He was with Joseph in a special way.

In the New Testament we read of Joseph, the earthly father of Jesus, who had several dreams from the Lord to give him direction for Jesus, Mary, and himself (Matthew 1–2). Peter had a vision from the Lord instructing him to go and minister to a group of Gentiles (Acts 10). While God uses these ways to communicate to us, we must discern which thoughts and dreams are from God. Certainly, most dreams are not from the Lord. My wife has a lot of crazy dreams that we laugh about together. There may be times we feel sure that what we are receiving is from the Lord; at other times, we are unsure, and should ask the Lord for confirmation if it is from Him, and what it might mean.

Sources of Thoughts and Ideas

There are several sources of thoughts and ideas that can influence us. These include God's leading through His Spirit, our own thoughts, and Satan's deceptions.

God and His Holy Spirit

God is faithful and will bring to pass what He says. He is greater than all of the lies and "noise" we have to put up with in life. His leading will always come to us through His Spirit, and He will make His will and direction clear to us if we will go to Him and wait on Him.

The Bible says, *"My sheep listen to my voice; I know them, and they follow me . . ."* (John 10:27).

Many say in this verse Jesus was talking about His followers when He was physically here. They could hear His voice as He spoke to them. But if it only refers to that time, it would imply that He no longer communicates with us by speaking to us. That would also imply we no longer have a need for Him to do so.

In John 14:26 it says, *"But the counselor, the Holy Spirit, whom the Father will send in my name, will teach you all things and will remind you of everything I have said to you."* John 16:15 also says, *"All that belongs to the Father is mine. That is why I said the Spirit will take from what is mine and make it known to you."* In fact, the Bible teaches us in many places that God wants to speak or communicate with His children. He primarily does this through His Word, the Bible, and through His Spirit, who lives in every believer or Christian.

I suggest a simple exercise. Get some paper and a pencil and begin to read His Word, praying over what you are reading. By this I mean whatever the Bible says that can be applicable to you, pray that God will make it real in your life or explain its meaning to you.

As you do this, write down the thoughts that come to you as you prayerfully read His Word. When you are done with the chapter you are reading, read the things you have written down. This simple exercise will open you up to hear from God's Spirit the things He desires to communicate or speak to you.

He will also expose any deceptions we may be entertaining or thinking about. He will cut through all the things that can confuse us and lead us astray, and He will bring truth to us. Again, *God is faithful, He is truth, and He is life.*

Our Thoughts

Of course, many of our thoughts come from ourselves. We can sometimes mistake the thoughts of our own hearts for God's thoughts or promptings. At times, these thoughts may seem to be good, moral, and seemingly beneficial; nevertheless, they may not be God's thoughts.

There are several sources of our thoughts:

Our own hearts. At times, it can be hard to distinguish between what God may be trying to tell us and what our hearts desire, which may or may not be of the Lord. The Bible says the heart is capable of being deceived (Proverbs 28:26, Jeremiah 17:7-10). Pride, selfishness, holding grudges, offenses, ambitions, the desire for recognition, laziness, or any number of other motivations lodged in our hearts can greatly influence us. This, in turn, can open us up to being misled. With that said, as we seek Him, He is faithful to reveal His will and will lead us.

Other people's opinions. We constantly get input in life. We must guard our hearts and minds and not let improper thoughts or philosophies take root (Proverbs 4:23). Many things we hear are either scripturally incorrect or bad advice. That is why we must choose our counselors carefully. I have heard of some people being advised to divorce their mates, make terrible business decisions, commit dishonest acts, and a number of other things that are simply baffling. Some of this counsel even came from those who call themselves Christians. Being grounded in God's Word helps us to be discerning and recognize good versus bad counsel.

The world's ideas. Certainly, the global culture and that of the United States are becoming more immoral and corrupt. While God is at work drawing many to Him, our culture is full of ungodly influences, philosophies, and values. Again, we must not allow those things to take root in our hearts and influence how we think (Colossians 2:6-8). Many get caught up in cultural or philosophical trends. It is important to remember we are in the world, but we are not to be of the world. We adhere to God's truth as taught in God's Word.

Deceiving Spirits

Just as God's Spirit can give us thoughts and impressions, so can the enemy. Satan is a deceiver and a liar and is out to destroy us if he can (John 8:44, 1 Peter 5:8). We must be aware that thoughts can come to us from Satan or other deceiving spirits. He can put thoughts in our minds to lead us astray, make us fearful, and deceive us. He will play on our weaknesses and use any form of temptation he can to cause us to fall into sin and bring harm to us and our families. He will lie about God, cause us to question God's true nature and faithfulness, and try to discourage us. That's why he is called "the destroyer."

Satan is not omnipresent (at all places at all times), nor can he read our minds. He and his forces (demons or seducing spirits) are trying to lead us astray. He will twist God's words to get us to succumb to temptation as he did with Eve in the Garden of Eden (Genesis 3). He will misquote Scripture, as he did with Jesus (Matthew 4:1-11). We must be "on alert" to his actions and ways (1 Peter 5:8), and knowing God's Word is what will help us distinguish between truth and error.

When I was living in Dallas, I met a young couple that was going through some real struggles. The husband, Tim, was a fairly new believer. As we talked, I became increasingly disturbed. Tim shared how his relationship with the Lord had "really grown." Of course, this sounded good to me. But then, he shared how the Lord was "leading" him to him to send out checks that he had no funds to cover. He was to do this "in faith," believing God would send the money. The checks bounced, and he was faced with fines and debt.

I asked him how he felt about this, and he said, "God had told him" not to question Him—that Tim did not need to understand; the important thing was his obedience. As this man shared other things, I became alarmed and encouraged him to come back to church and get into a men's group. I told him there were seasoned men there with whom he could share his life and who could disciple him. He responded in a proud manner that if a man wanted to disciple him, that man should call and offer to do so. He should not have to pursue anyone to guide him.

I told him that at times, we can be misled or deceived even though we are sincere. We should measure direction against God's Word and sound biblical counsel. He let me know he knew "God's voice" and didn't need input from others.

I again appealed to him, but to no avail.

This story, while true, is very sad. God certainly would not have directed Tim to write bad checks. God can provide before we write the check, so our witness and reputation remain intact. The Bible says that we are to *"have a good reputation with those outside the church, so that [we] will not fall into reproach and the snare of the devil"* (1 Timothy 3:7).

While this Scripture addresses a necessary qualification for a church leader, it is obviously true for all believers. We may make mistakes, but we do not purposely do things that can bring reproach (bad reputation) upon us. If Tim would have checked his direction with God's Word or wise counsel, he would have questioned his "leading," and he could have abandoned his unwise decisions.

Pride can be a downfall, including being spiritually prideful. We may think we have the corner on knowing God and don't need input from others. Satan wants to isolate us and keep us from wise counsel and discernment.

Such unfortunate stories should not discourage us from pursing direction from God. Anytime God is moving, Satan and his forces are there to try to disrupt what God is doing. However, if we are seeking Him and are reading His Word, and willing to seek godly counsel, these types of deceptions can be stopped. We do need to have godly caution, but not be motivated by fear. God is near and is always faithful.

Wise Discernment

Thoughts can come from all of the above sources. Even though we will need to grow in our ability to discern, we can trust that God will keep us and guide us into all truth as we:

- renew our minds, as He tells us (Romans 12:2),
- ask Him to change our hearts, as He desires to (Psalm 51:10, 119:32; Jeremiah 24:7), and
- walk humbly before Him, as He commands (Micah 6:8).

While we must be on the alert so we are not misled, the Bible states clearly that when we seek God and cry out to Him, He will respond and give us the insight and leadership we need. It may come right away or over time as we seek Him. At times, God does not answer us right away. In those cases, we should wait until we are sure we have His direction. Godly caution is a good thing. It does not mean we do nothing out of fear of being wrong—it means we wait for His assurance, which He will give us.

Godly caution regarding potential direction we are discerning is not unbelief. A lack of caution can be foolish and lead to making impulsive and irresponsible decisions. Waiting on God and getting wise guidance can lead to safety. Many times, when the decisions are important and we are unsure what course to take, we should ask God to confirm His leading to us. This is not a lack of faith. It is better to get confirmation and be sure, than to plunge ahead and find out later we were wrong.

God does not reveal everything to us at once. He gives us direction and, as we move forward, He continues to give us light, or understanding. His purpose is for us to continue to seek Him to get the ongoing direction we need. Our relationship with Him is to be continual, and He supplies what we need as we go. (At times, mid-course adjustments are in order as we get more understanding.)

Big Assignments

As you walk with God through life, He may give you a big assignment. One you think you cannot do. But God can do it through you. He will do it; you just have to move forward as He gives direction. Do your part, and watch Him bring it to pass. There are many stories in the Bible of God giving assignments that men thought they could not do, but as they obeyed God, He brought it to pass as they ventured out.

Gideon is a good example in Judges 6–8. An angel showed up and said to him, *"The Lord is with you, O mighty man of valor"* (Judges 6:12). I'm sure Gideon looked around to see who he was speaking to. Gideon responded:

"Please, my Lord, if the Lord is with us, why then has all this happened to us? And where are all His wonderful deeds that our fathers recounted to us, saying, 'Did not the Lord bring us up for Egypt?' But now the Lord has forsaken us and given us into the hand of Midian." The angel responded, *"Go in this might of yours and save Israel from the hand of Midian; do not I send you?"* Gideon responded, *"Please Lord, how can I save Israel? Behold, my clan is the weakest in Manasseh, and I am the least in my father's house."* The angel replied,

"But I will be with you, and you shall strike the Midianites as one man." (Judges 6:13–16)

Gideon wanted to see Israel delivered, but he did not think God could do it through him. He looked at himself and said, "Naw, no way." Often, we look at our own shortcomings and think God cannot use us, especially to accomplish anything of consequence. There is a good saying: "God does not call the qualified, but qualifies the called." God often does not use those who think they can do it because they are so gifted, talented, or trained. He instead calls those who rely on Him and trust in Him to get it done. They are willing to do their part but realize God is blessing their efforts and causing the task to be completed.

The story goes on the say that Gideon surrendered to God and a great victory was won. To make sure He got the glory, God had Gideon dismiss 31,700 men and go into battle with just 300. The enemy was tens of thousands strong, and by anyone's standards, all bets were on the enemy winning against Gideon. But God worked a miracle, the victory was won, and Israel was set free from the Midianites.

While we may not be chosen to lead a battle, God nevertheless wants to give us tasks greater than we think we can accomplish. He is looking for surrendered vessels to work through.

God gave Gideon guidance as he obeyed. Each step, God gave him directions of His plan to accomplish what He had called Gideon to do.

God is faithful. He will always be with you and guide you to accomplish His calling.

QUESTIONS FOR REFLECTION AND DISCUSSION

1. Have you ever been in a situation where you wanted to do something but were uneasy because you were unsure about it agreeing with God's Word? If so, what did you do? What was the outcome?

   _____

   _____

   _____

   _____

2. Have you ever thought God was leading a certain way but were unsure whether it was really Him, whether it was your own thoughts and desires—or whether you were even being misled? If so how did you go about discerning?

   _____

   _____

   _____

   _____

3. Looking back to that situation, is there anything you would do differently if the situation were to arise again? If so, what?

   _____

   _____

   _____

   _____

   _____

4. Do you have confidence that if you seek God He will respond? If not, why not?

_____

_____

_____

_____

TAKE A KNEE

Let's pray: *"Father, create in me a desire to seek You and Your leadership in all areas of my life. If pride or stubbornness is an issue in my life, change me that I might live before You in a manner that is pleasing to You. Teach me Your ways. Renew my mind to think the way You desire. Keep me from deception and being led astray. I commit my life to You."*

Chapter 4

Confirmation and Timing

God delights to confirm His will and leading to us. He may do this in any number of ways: through others, through our pastors' messages, through circumstances, or other means. I have often asked God to confirm His will to me when I was unsure of my course of action and the outcome was important. He always has.

God's Confirmation

There are several checks that help us discern if our leading and direction is from God.

The cornerstone of Scripture. As we have seen, the primary way is to compare all direction with the truth of God's Word. God's written Word is the cornerstone to compare all teaching, counsel, and direction against. If it does not agree with Scripture, it is not from the Lord.

Our wives. For those of us who are married, it is important to talk with our wives and pray together about all major life decisions. God will often use her either to confirm or to give caution. In her spirit, she may feel a peace and "green light" to move ahead or a check or alarm about moving forward. Many men have been spared potentially disastrous consequences by asking for their wife's discernment and advice.

Certainly, in all family matters, husbands and wives should talk and pray together about direction. Ideally, both a man and his wife should have agreement and peace about decisions and direction. If a man believes he is to act contrary to his wife's counsel, it should be with caution, with prayer, and after getting other wise advice. Many men refuse to move forward on a major decision until they are in agreement with their wives. They are trusting God to work in both of them to confirm His direction.

Godly advisors. We can also go to wise friends or mentors, tell them the direction we are considering, and trust them to help us discern. Most wise advisors will not tell us what to do. They realize the final decision is up to us. Sometimes, when I have given counsel, if it is clear people are getting ready to embark on something unscriptural or unwise, I will tell them that. At times, I have strongly encouraged people to do or not do something, when I felt compelled to do so for their own good.

However, often an advisor will help you consider the decision in light of Scripture and wise business and a practical outlook. Then, they may pray with you that God will make it clear. Often, discussing this with another will bring clarity. At other times, a lack of clarity means to wait until the Lord makes it clear. This is godly caution and God honors that.

In addition to these ways, I have learned that God's direction brings God's peace. Because *peace* is such a prevalent theme in Scripture and is significant, let's look at this word and its meaning in more depth.

God's Peace

In the Old Testament, the Hebrew word translated "peace" is *shalom*. It literally means "to be secure, at ease and safe; to have a sense of well-being; to be 'complete.'" In the New Testament, peace comes from a Greek word meaning "to be undisturbed; to have a sense of welfare." Webster's Dictionary defines peace as "freedom from disturbance or inner turmoil."

In Isaiah 9:6, Jesus is called the "Prince of Peace." This is not an empty title. Peace of heart and soul is part of the believer's inheritance. When we accept Christ as our Savior, we accept the very Prince of Peace into our lives.

Jesus spoke peace to others. When Jesus forgave sins or healed, He often said, "Go in peace" (Mark 5:34; Luke 7:50, 8:48). When He sent out His disciples, He told them to bring a blessing of peace to the homes in which they stayed (Luke 10:5). Jesus told His disciples,

> *Peace I leave with you; My peace I give to you; not as the world gives do I give to you. Do not let your heart be troubled, nor let it be fearful. (John 14:27)*

> *These things I have spoken to you, so that in Me you may have peace. In the world you have tribulation, but take courage; I have overcome the world. (John 16:33)*

The apostles, in their writings, also spoke peace to the believers. Almost every New Testament epistle opens with a greeting in which the author asks God to grant the readers "grace" and "peace" (see Romans 1:7; 1 Corinthians 1:3; 2 Corinthians 1:2).

Obviously, peace is a gift from God to bring joy and tranquility to our hearts and souls. This does not mean we will not experience difficulty or hardship, or at times be troubled. But God desires to give us His peace despite our circumstances.

Jesus did not want us to live in anxiety and worry. He said,

> *Therefore do not be anxious, saying, "What shall we eat?" or "What shall we drink?" or "What shall we wear?" For the Gentiles seek after all these things, and your heavenly Father knows that you need them all. But seek first the kingdom of God and his righteousness, and all these things will be added to you. (Matthew 6:31-33)*

It is impossible to have true peace when we are worrying and fearful. Often, when we are in turmoil, God's Spirit assures us as we pray that all is well, and He is present in our circumstances. As we believe that, our hope and faith return, and can once again know peace. Anxiety and worry not only bring emotional turmoil, but can also bring physical problems and sickness (ever had a headache after worrying about something?). But, the peace Jesus left us is to be a part of our lives. It is always available for the taking.

At times, during adverse circumstances, we may be in turmoil. We need to pray, give the circumstances to God, and begin to confess that God is faithful and all will work out. If we hold onto the "what ifs" and dwell upon the negative, we will not have peace. The enemy will feed our mind with negative thoughts and try to harass us and take our peace. But we can chose to trust God, believe Him, and not allow our thoughts to dwell on negative outcomes. There are times God will give us a supernatural peace and other times we must chose to trust God and commit our circumstances to Him, no matter how uncomfortable it may feel.

There was a time, when the economy fell apart, that one of my lenders filed a lawsuit against me for money owed to them. It was for several million dollars, and I did not have the money or feel I owed it. I lay in bed one night contemplating how the outcome could bankrupt me and praying about it. The Lord challenged me to trust Him, do all He led me to do, and leave the outcome to Him. I could be at peace or I could worry and live an anxious, fretting life until this was settled. I realized God did not want me to live an anxious, worrying, fretting life, so I chose to trust in Him for the outcome. I continued to pray about it, as did my wife, and when the enemy tried to make me worry or fret, I chose to trust God and put it in His hands. The majority of the time, I had peace that all would turn out okay.

This process lasted about a year, and eventually, it was settled for pennies on the dollar. I walked away free from this and went forward. God guided me through this. I received godly counsel from a number of sources, including my attorney, and all was settled. God was faithful: He worked on my behalf and showed His delivering power. It was a test for me to trust God, obey Him, and see Him deliver me.

The redemptive work Jesus did on the cross for us, and the love He has for us, assures us He will never leave us or forsake us. His promises are true for us and for all who believe. Regardless of our past mistakes or problems, God is there for us.

God was faithful to all of His promises to Israel even though they were obstinate and rebellious. He was faithful to His word (Joshua 21:45, 1 Kings 8:56). Satan tries to lie to us and tell us God cannot be trusted, or His promises are not for us because we do not deserve them. His desire is to steal our peace and replace it with turmoil, worry, fear, and doubt.

Isaiah 26:3 says, *"The steadfast of mind You will keep in perfect peace, because he trusts in You."* So, we can have peace through all circumstances because we trust in God and His promises. What does having peace have to do with guidance and direction? Since Jesus gives us peace, we should pay attention when we feel lingering doubt, uncertainty, or even a "check" in our spirits. This lack of peace may indicate our direction is wrong or we should not take the direction we are contemplating. Or, it can indicate that we are not trusting the Lord and are being hassled by the enemy. The Lord is faithful to show us which it is.

Philippians 4:6-7 states, *"Be anxious for nothing, but in everything by prayer and supplication with thanksgiving let your requests be made known to God. And the peace of God, which surpasses all comprehension, will guard your hearts and your minds in Christ Jesus."* When we make our requests known to God, His peace will be upon us. This happens as we are able to trust the outcome to Him. However, if what we are asking for or the decision we have made is not God's will, we will not have peace in our spirits. If God is not giving His peace, there is a problem.

There have been times I thought God was leading me in a certain direction. However, as I began to pursue that direction, I felt uneasy. When this has happened, my wife and I prayed together and told the Lord that we needed peace from Him, or we would stop our present course until we did have His peace.

The apostle Paul, in Acts 16, determined several times to go to Bithynia but *"the Spirit of Jesus did not allow them"* (Acts 16:7). Afterwards, Paul received a vision telling him to go to Macedonia. As he waited on God, the direction became clear.

At times, we may have a short window of opportunity to make a decision. We should be cautious in these circumstances. Pray over the decision; make sure you believe it is the right thing to do. If there is not peace or if there is doubt, then it is best to wait. A good rule to follow regarding a major decision is that if you do not have time to consider something carefully, to wait on God, and to get good counsel, then you should let the opportunity pass. Being pressured to make any major decision is not wise. By refusing to make hasty decisions, I personally have been spared what turned out to be bad opportunities.

God's peace follows God's direction. This is one way to confirm God's direction.

God's Timing

Timing can also be a crucial issue in God's leading us, and our decision-making processes. In fact, God's timing can be as important as God's direction. There are many instances we may believe we are to do something, but the way seems blocked.

We need to pray and search out God in these times. He has His own timing and reasons for wanting us to wait, which we may not understand. He may not give us a reason, but simply lead us to wait on Him. Trust is all important in these times. Possibly, God wants to accomplish something in a way we cannot. Or, He may be preparing us for the task ahead.

Such was the case with Moses. At age forty, Moses felt called by God to help deliver his people, the Israelites, from the bondage of Egypt. His human attempt resulted in murder, and he fled Egypt for his life. He then spent forty years as a shepherd before God supernaturally called and equipped him to deliver the Israelites from Egypt.

Moses had grown up in Pharaoh's house, been educated by royal tutors, and lived a life of privilege. He had favor and position. From a natural viewpoint, Moses seemed quite capable of carrying out the mission God had for him. However, God wanted to train Moses in His school and prepare him in His way. Forty years passed before God called Moses to fulfill the mission he originally felt called to do (Exodus 2–4). FORTY YEARS!

While we may not have to wait that long, God has His timing—and it is not always ours. We don't want to try to accomplish God's will in our ways. Sometimes we have to wait (which help us to develop virtues such as patience and understanding). He may want to involve others for their benefit, or do it in such a way that we know it was His doing and not ours. Therefore, God will get the glory, not us. Regardless, when we are waiting on Him, He will make it clear when the time is right.

I have told the Lord a number of times that He didn't understand my plans and my program. When I have felt God wasn't answering my prayers as He ought, or things were not happening as I thought they should, I have told my wife that God needed to "get with it" and get on my program. We would both laugh. He has His program and His timing. Often, His are nothing like my own.

QUESTIONS FOR REFLECTION AND DISCUSSION

1. If you have a decision you are currently making, what confirmation have you received from Scripture, your wife, or godly advisors?

CONFIRMATION AND TIMING

2. Are there any areas of this decision in which you are lacking peace? If so, to what do you attribute this lack of peace (e.g., general anxiety, insecurity, a godly caution, fear, wise discernment)?

___

3. What core thoughts have you learned in this study that you want to be sure to remember?

___

4. Do you believe God will give you wisdom, guidance, and direction if you seek Him for it? Can you give Scripture for this? If so, help solidify your thinking by writing out your answer below.

___

TAKE A KNEE

Let's pray: *"Father, put in me a desire to follow You and Your direction. Help me to be open to hearing Your 'voice' and recognizing Your leadership in my life. Teach me Your ways. Put in me a hunger to read the Bible. I pray Your Spirit will not leave me alone, but prompt me daily to pray and seek You. I ask You for wisdom, guidance, and understanding. I confess that I need Your leadership. Give me eyes to see Your activity and ears to hear Your guidance. Grant it to me, I pray."*

A FINAL WORD

It is a sign of wisdom, not weakness, to inquire of the Lord for guidance. In desiring direction from God, we should practice the following steps:

1. Do your "due diligence—" your homework. Gather the necessary information to consider the decision or direction. List the positives and negatives, the "up" side and "down" side risks.
2. Ask God to grant you wisdom, understanding, and discernment.
3. Ask God to show you any improper motives you may have. Ask Him to give you a right heart with Him in seeking for direction.
4. Study God's Word for wisdom and direction.
5. Pray daily, asking God to give you His direction. Pray specifically about decisions you need to make. If it is an important or critical decision, consider a time of prayer and fasting
6. Get godly counsel when needed or in doubt.
7. If married, ask for your wife's counsel and pray with her.
8. Use godly caution. Don't move forward until you believe you should.
9. Make sure you have peace in your spirit from God about your direction.
10. Make sure your timing is right. If it is, it will work out.

A FINAL WORD

There is no question God leads us to do things that would fail without His provision and help. He often leads us to do things that may seem impossible, and that we know we cannot accomplish without Him. If He is leading you that way, He will be faithful to help you accomplish what He desires you to do. At times, He leads us to do things that seem scary and too big for us. But He is always faithful and always with us. Where God guides, He provides.

Finally, remember that you are a child of God and fully entitled to His leadership because He promised to give it. You can move with confidence and assurance as the Lord leads you, knowing He is with you and will help you in all you do.

ABOUT THE AUTHOR

Lou Turner wrote the "Living Life God's Way" series out of his passion for men to discover God, and to get to know Him and what He has for them. This 13-book men's discipleship series is the culmination of Lou's own journey—a life of seeking God, studying His Word, memorizing Scripture and meditating on it, and practical experience with family, community, marketplace work, and Christian ministry. It also comes, by Lou's own admission, from life experiences of both successes and mistakes, as a result of both good and bad decisions.

Lou has headed ministries, written and taught workshops, classes, and seminars, and discipled dozens of men. Now, he has put into print the things he has learned to help other men along their path and journey.

Most of Lou's growing up years were spent in Detroit and its suburbs, where he was raised in a pastor's home. Following his graduation from university with a Bachelor of Science in Business Administration, Lou and his wife planted and pastored a church for three years. After that time, he felt the strong call of God to return to business.

Over the years, Lou has served in numerous senior executive positions with national and international companies in the real estate and oil and gas industries. As of this writing, Lou is still active in business with his own home building company. He has

ABOUT THE AUTHOR

been married to his wife Joan since they were 20. They have three children and 10 grandchildren and make their home in Phoenix, Arizona.

www.ingramcontent.com/pod-product-compliance
Lightning Source LLC
Chambersburg PA
CBHW021123080526
44587CB00010B/623